This book belongs to

ABC's of the BIBLE COLORING BOOK

By Masheik Bassham

Scribbler's Press
(615) 635-7650

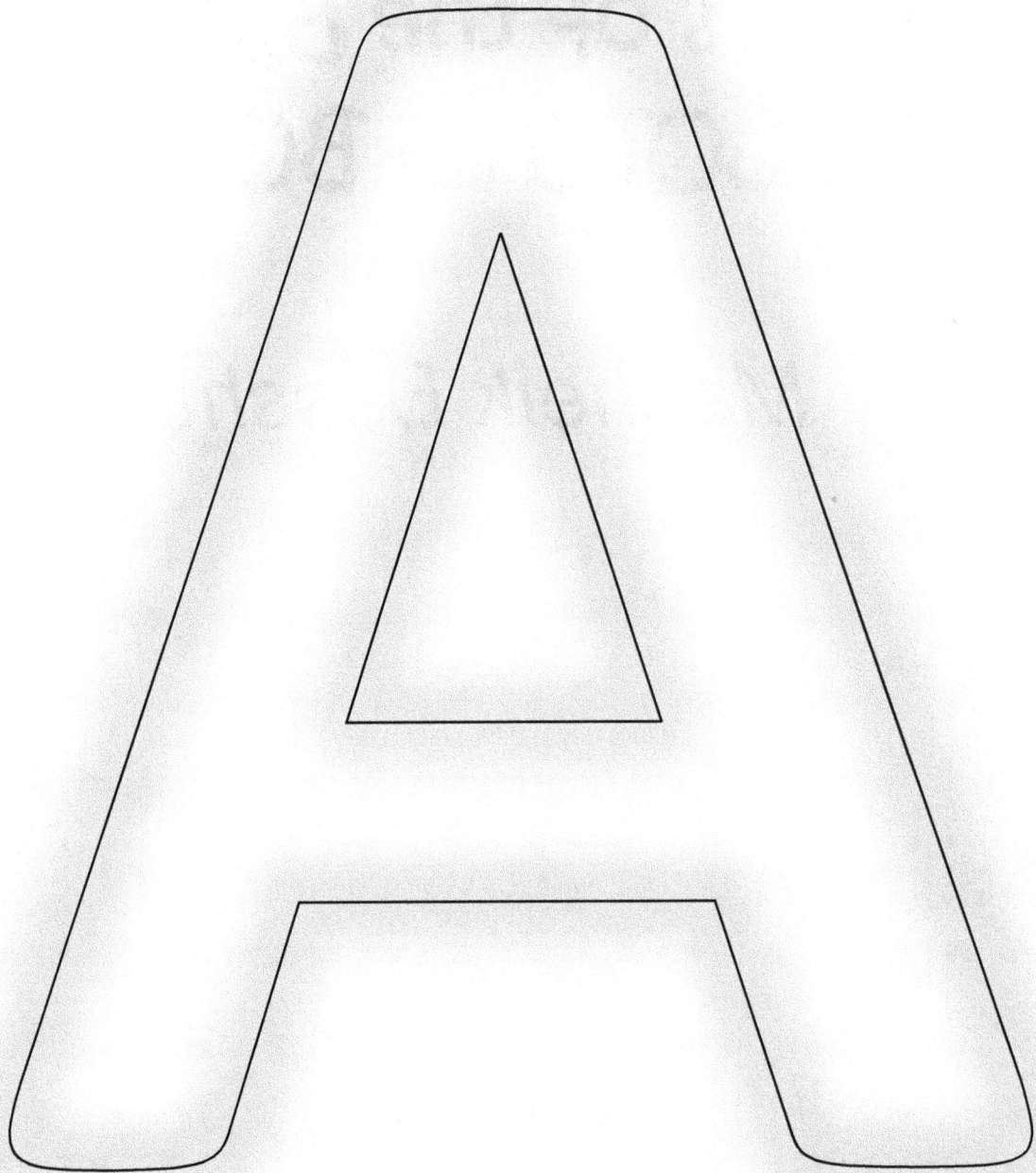

A

Abraham

He was the father of many nations.

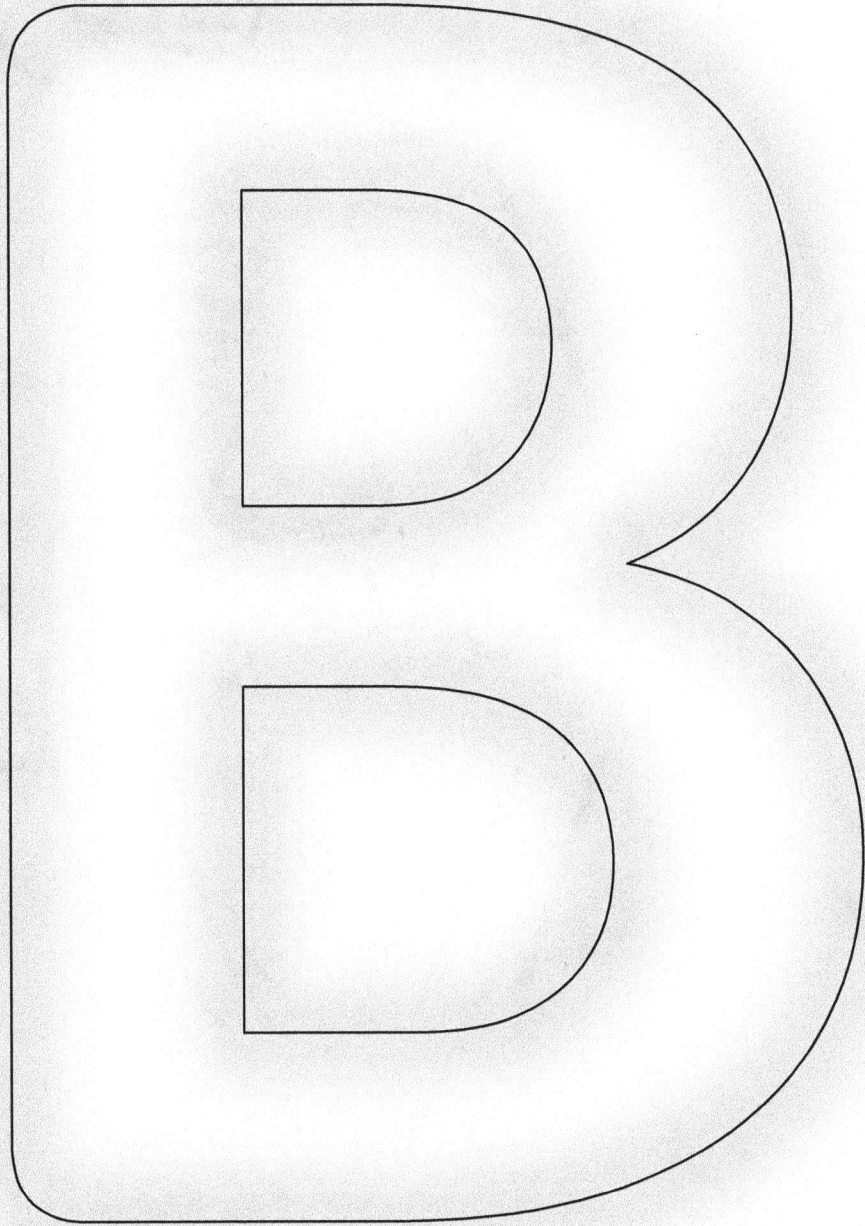

B

Bethlehem

The city where Jesus was born.

C

Church

House of worship

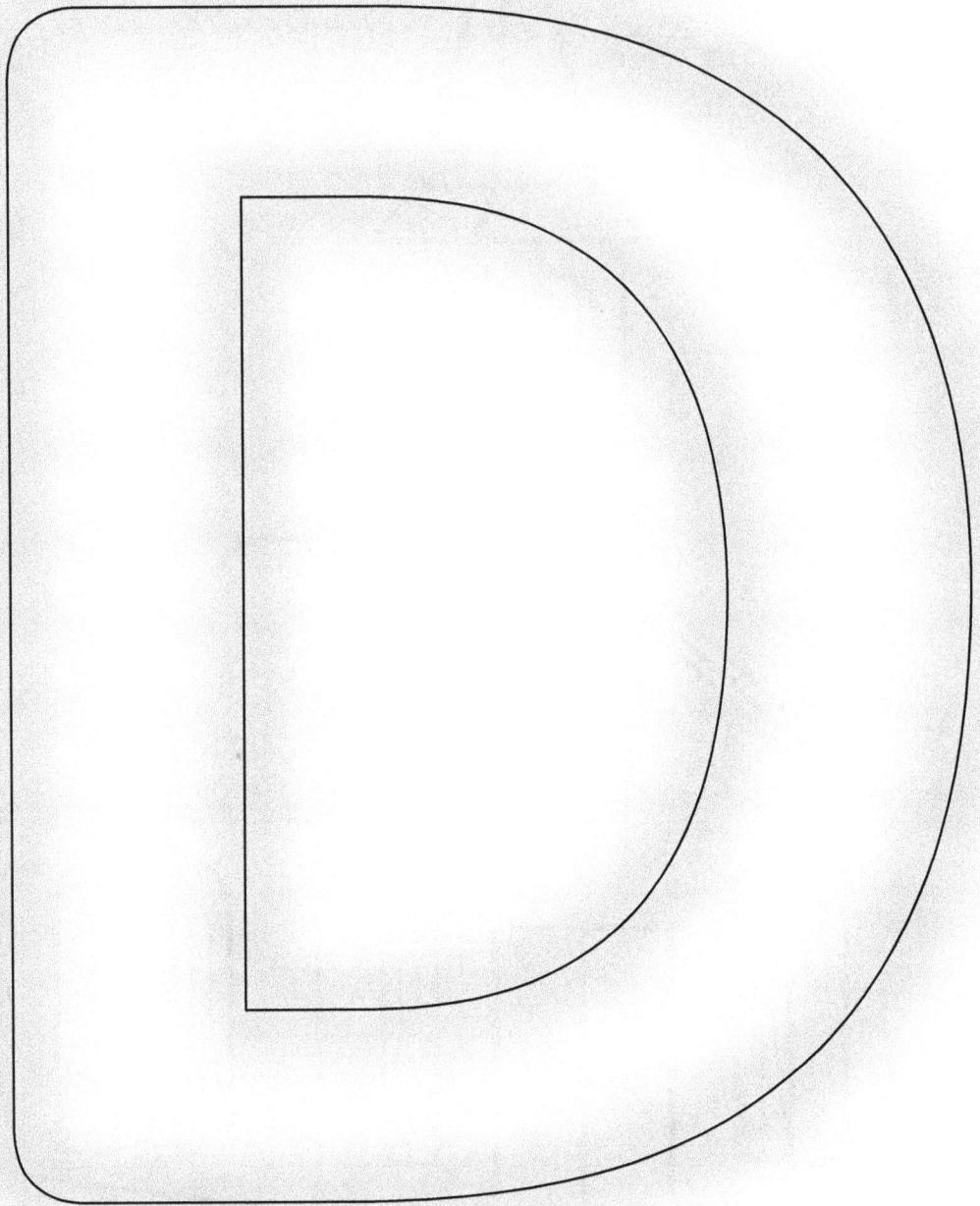

Daniel

Daniel in the lions' den

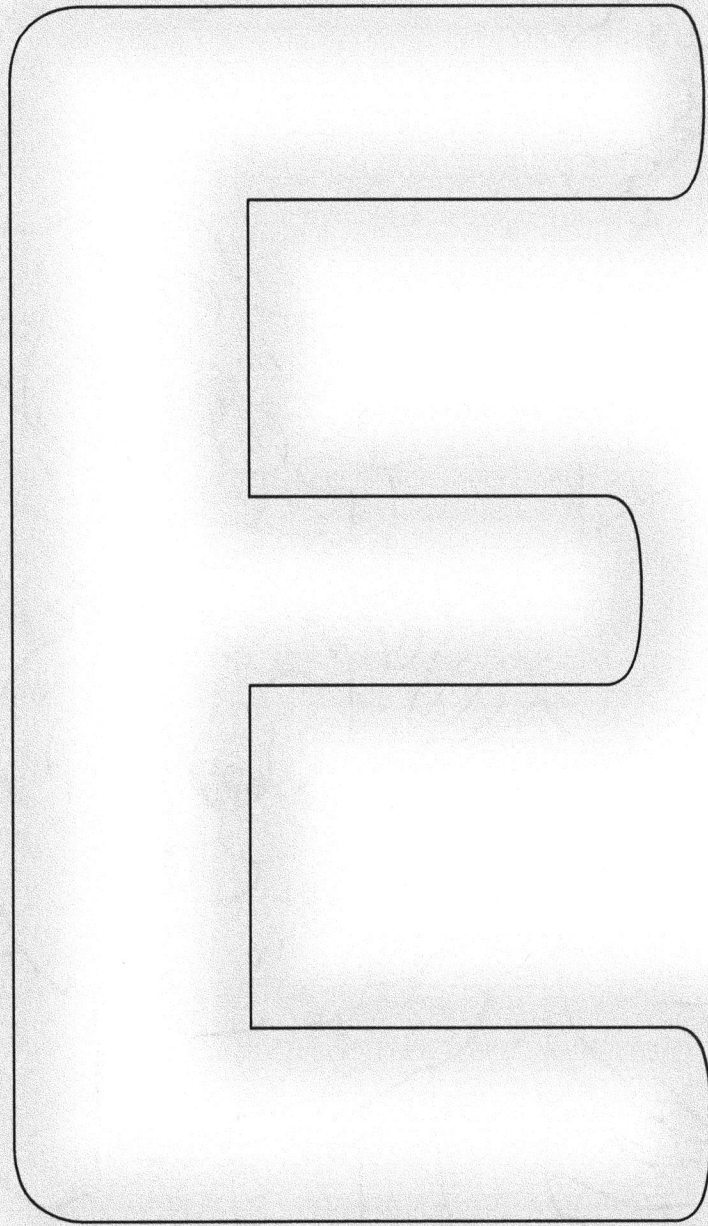

E

Eve

Adam and Eve in the Garden of Eden

F

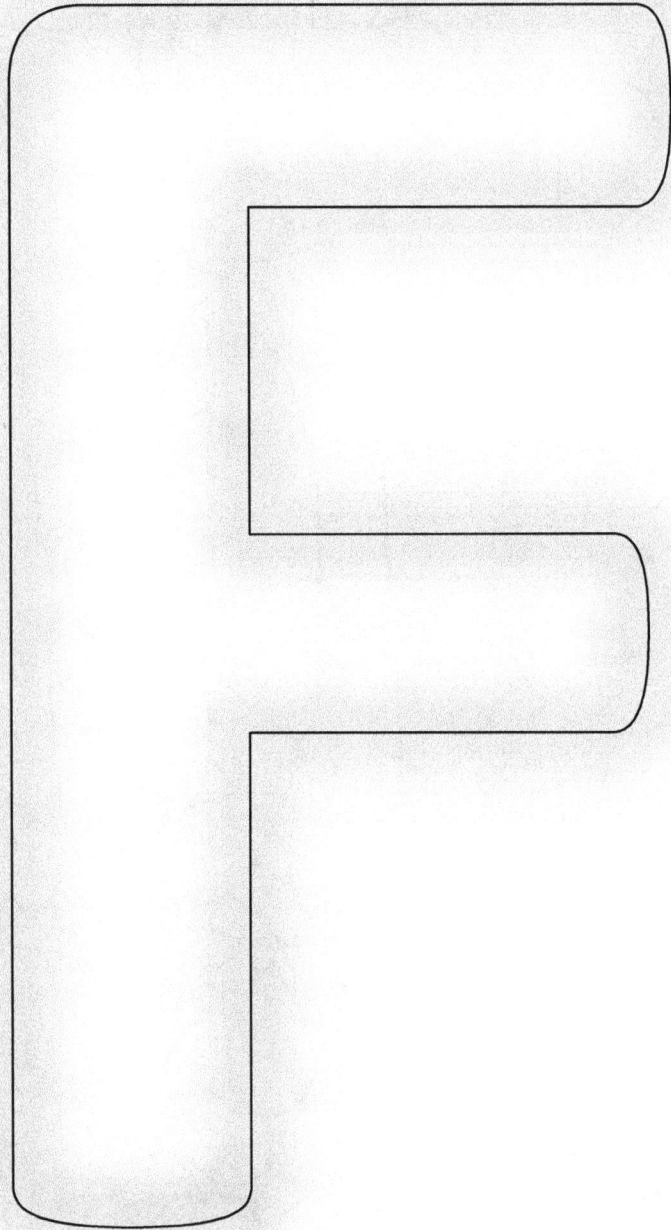

Fiery Furnace

The three Hebrew boys were thrown into a fiery furnace by the King but were rescued by God.

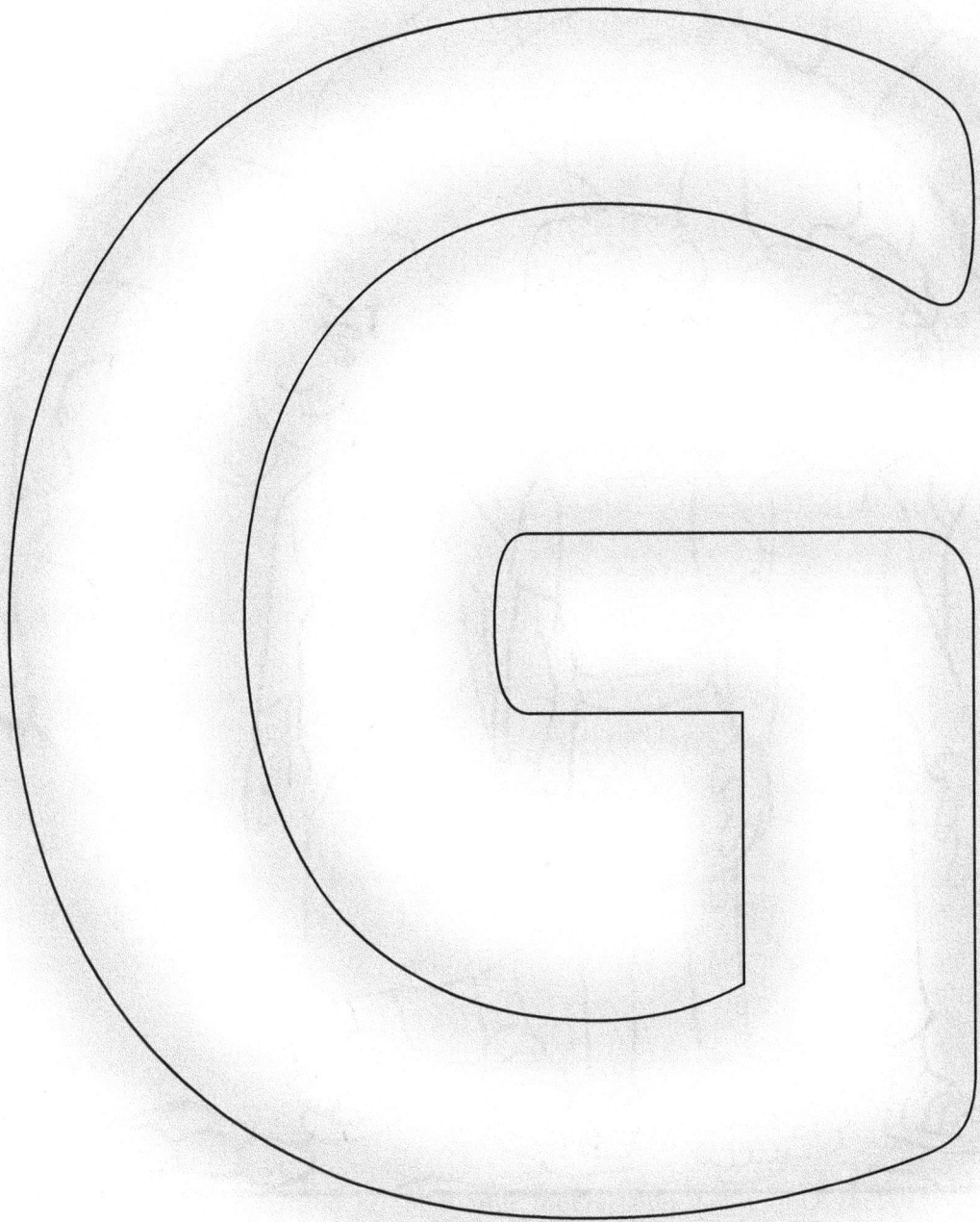

G

Goliath

David defeated Goliath.

H

Heaven

The gateway to Heaven

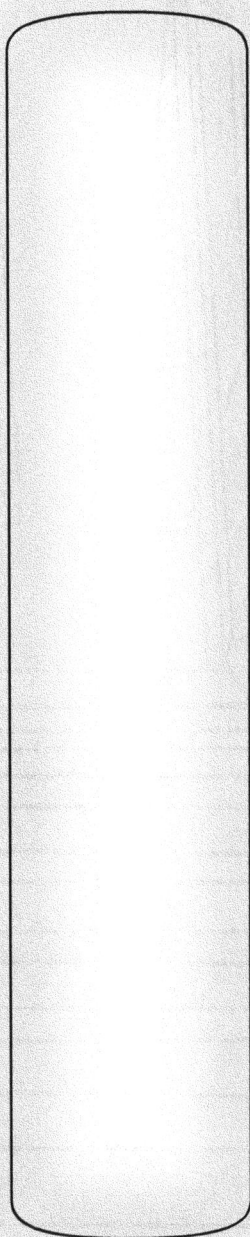

Image

I love who God created.

Jesus

The Son of God

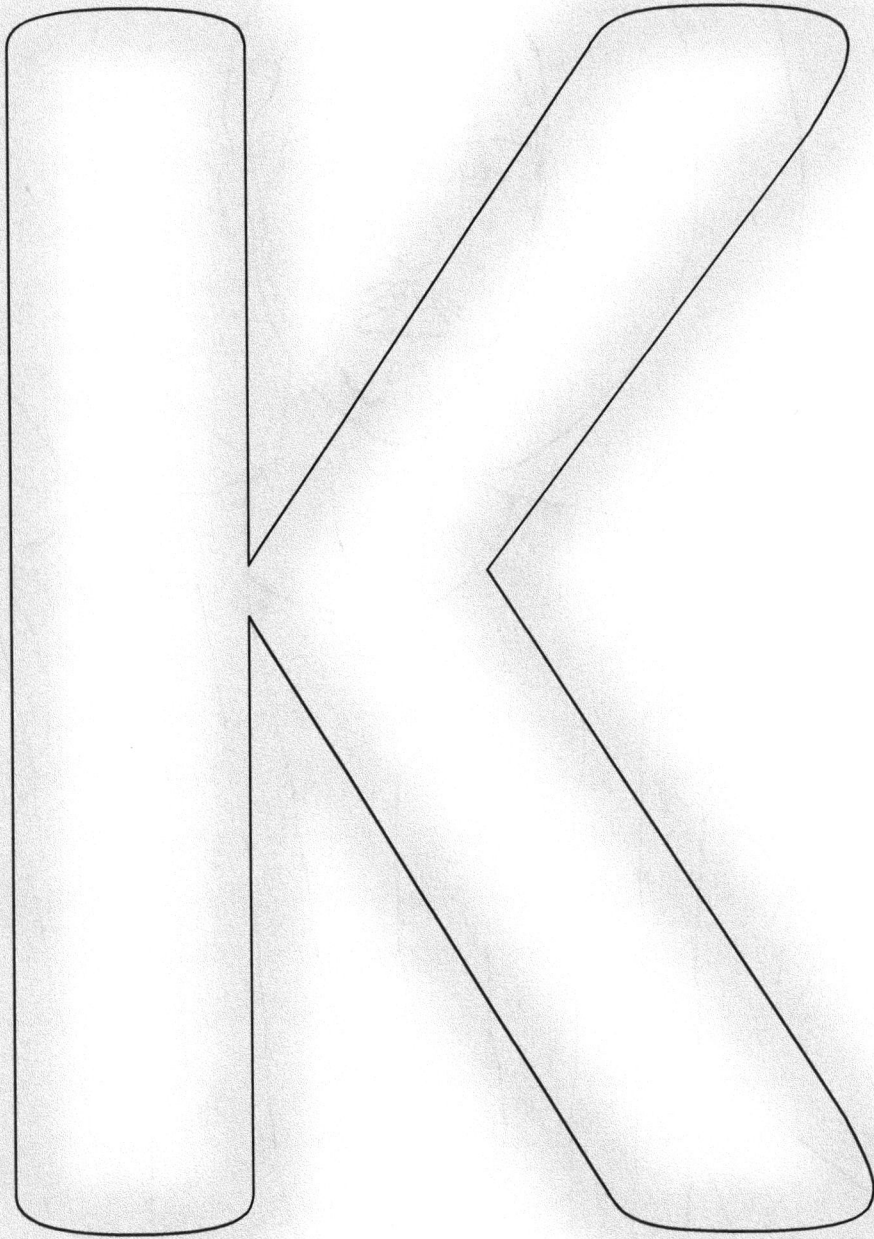

K

King Solomon

He was great in wisdom,
wealth, and power.

L

Lamb

Jesus, the Lamb of God, was sacrificed for our sin.

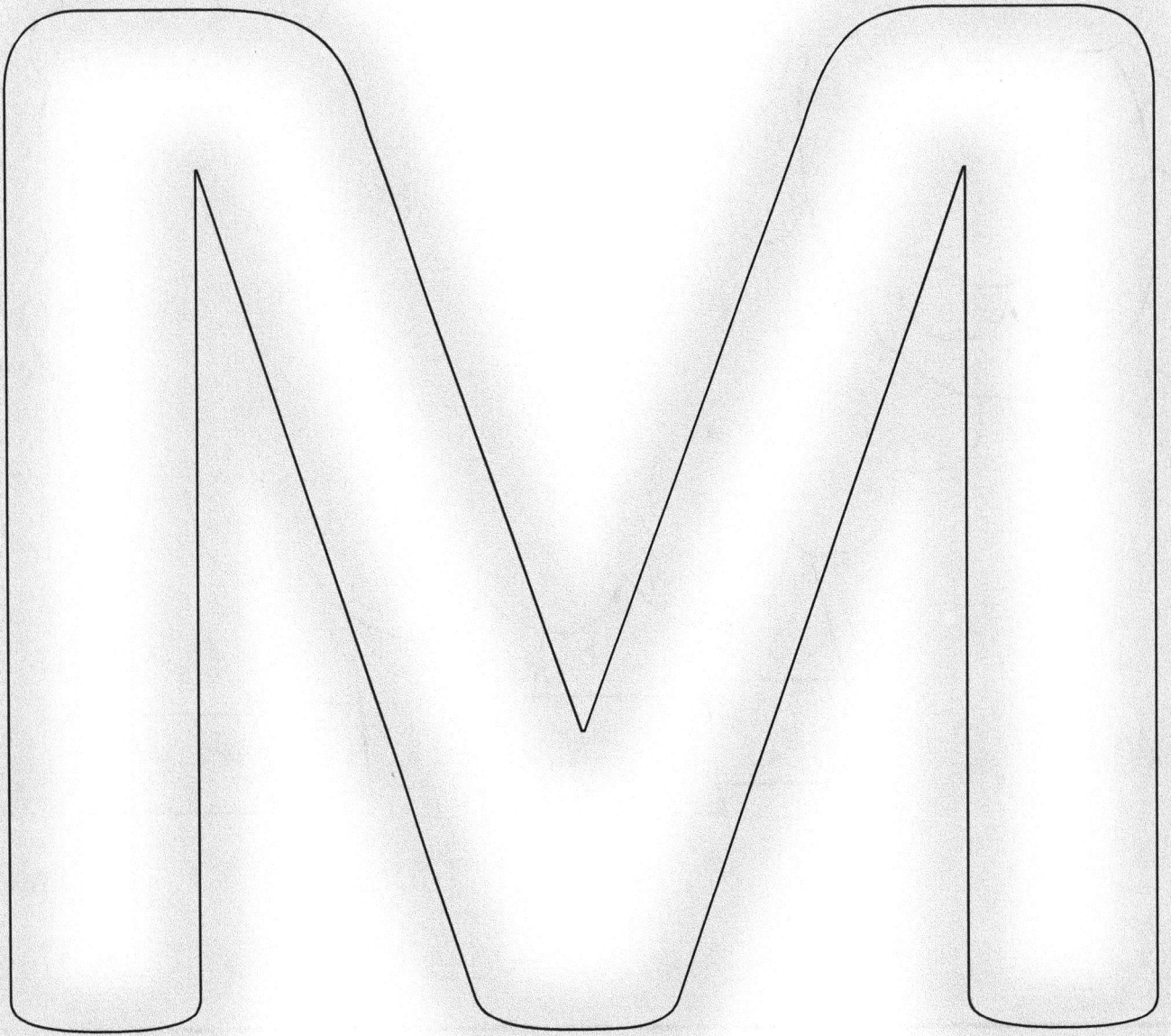

M

Moses

Moses led his people to freedom.

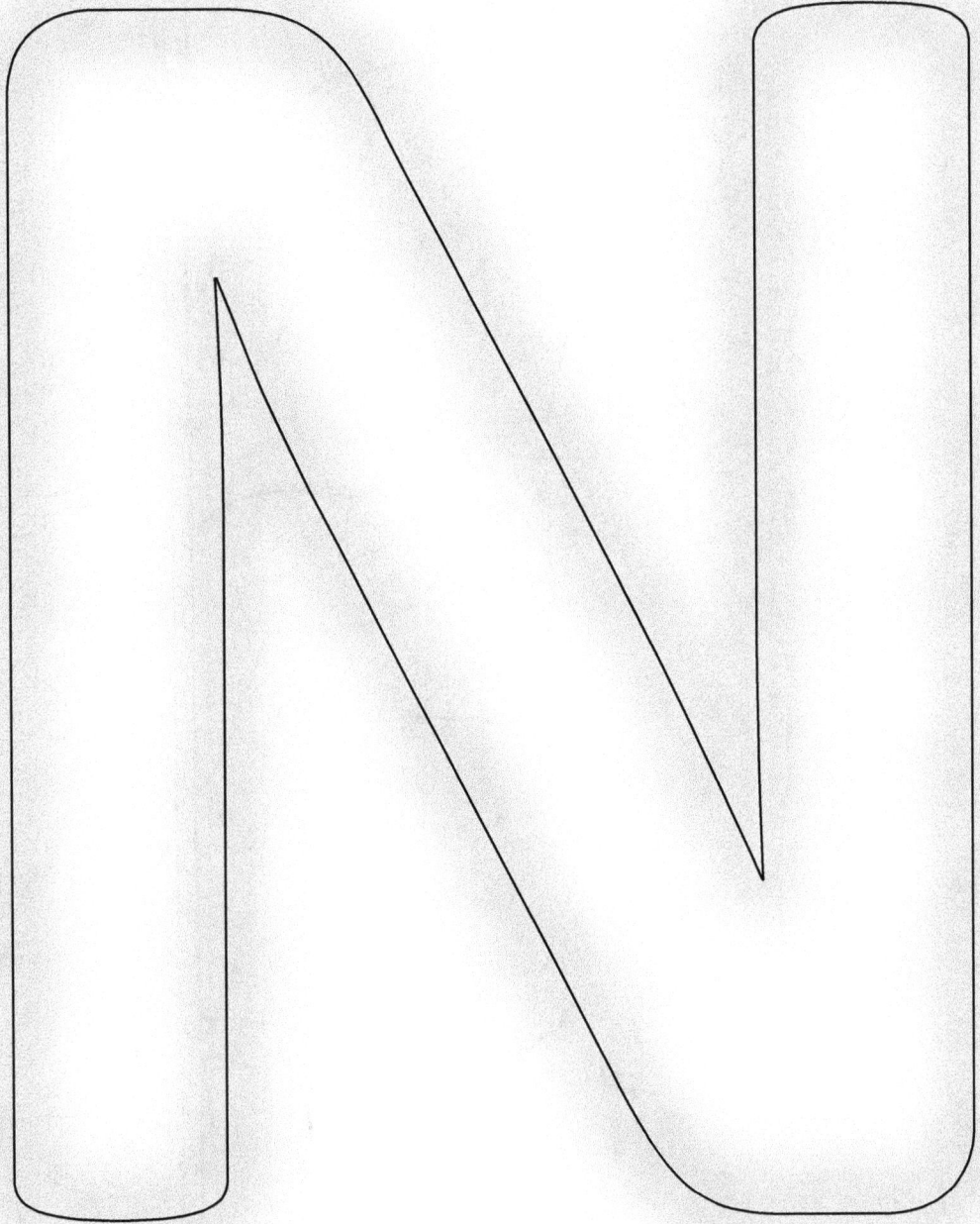

N

Nativity

Mary, Joseph, and the baby Jesus in a manger.

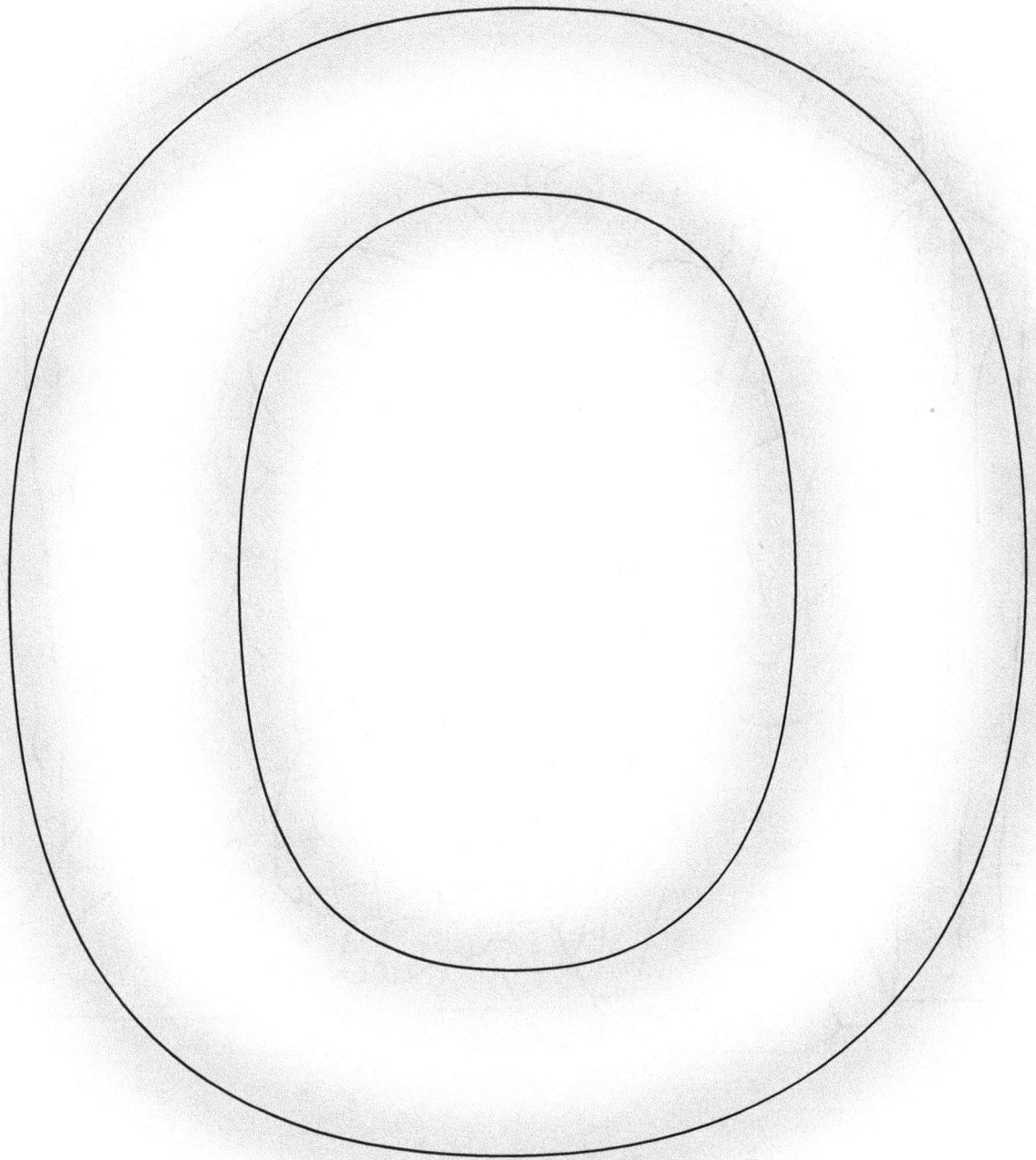

O

Olive Tree

Olive trees represent fruitfulness, richness, anointing, and brilliance.

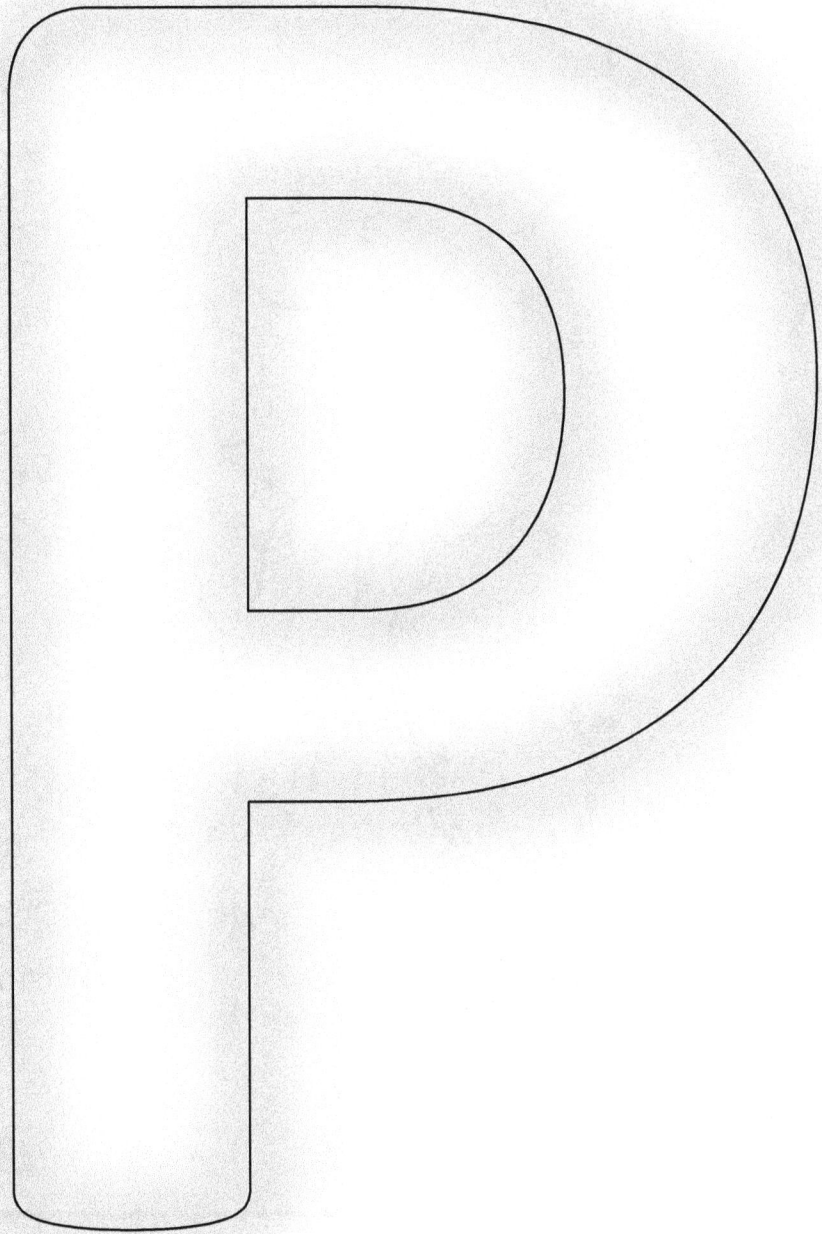

Prayer

Talk to God through prayer.

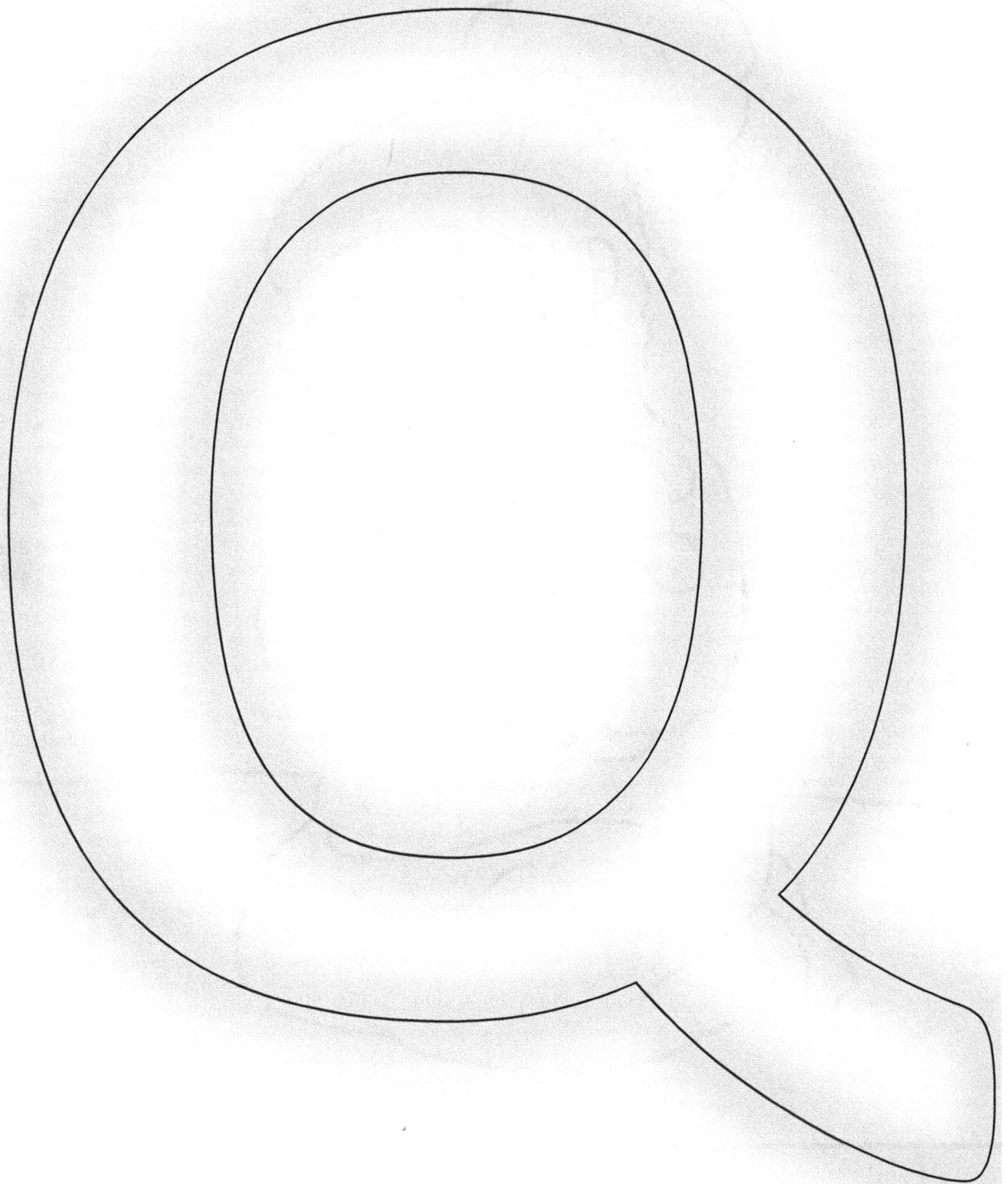

Q

Queen Esther

She saved the Jews, who
were God's people.

R

Rainbow

The rainbow reminds God of His promise to the world.

Star

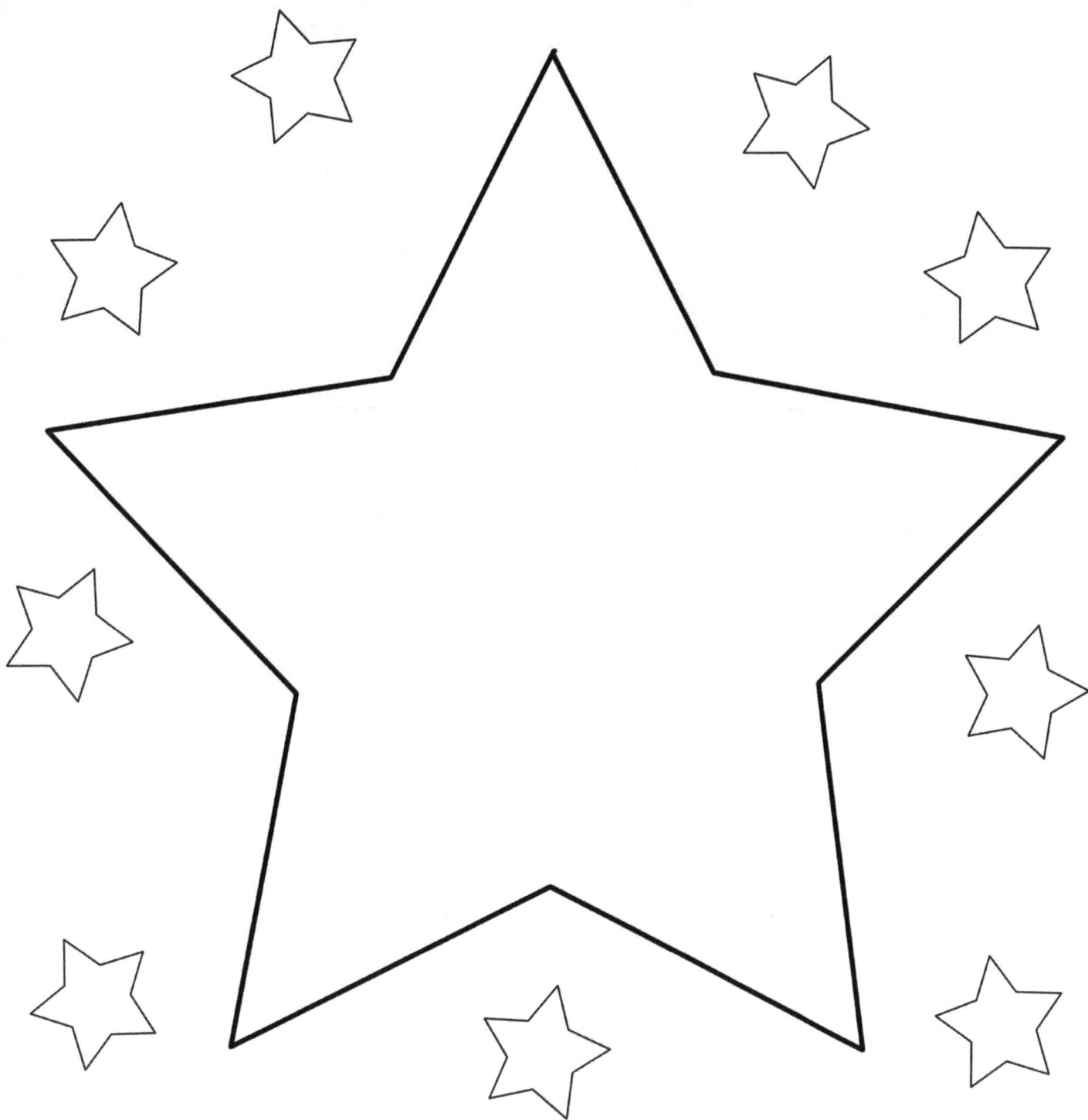

A star led the shepherds to Jesus.

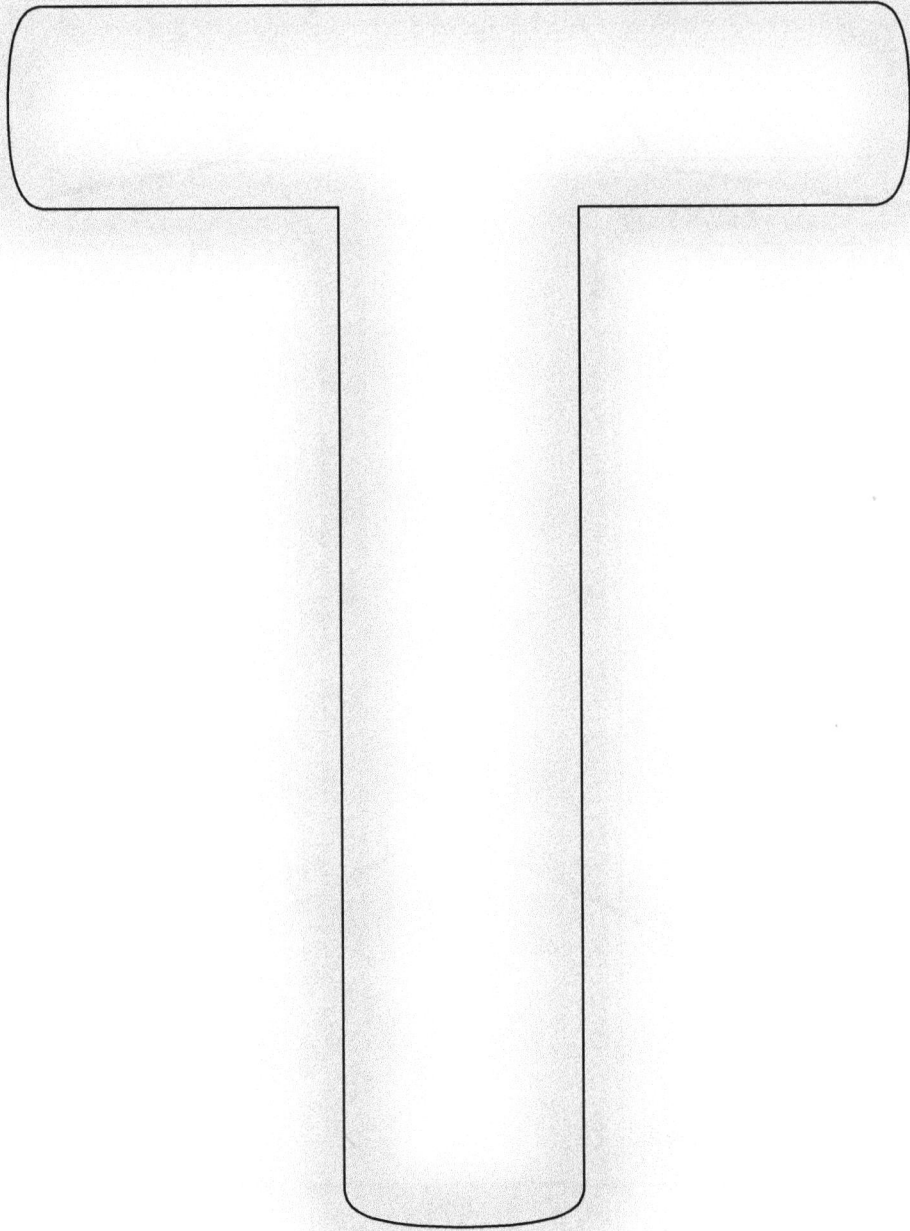

T

Timothy

He was Paul's young helper.

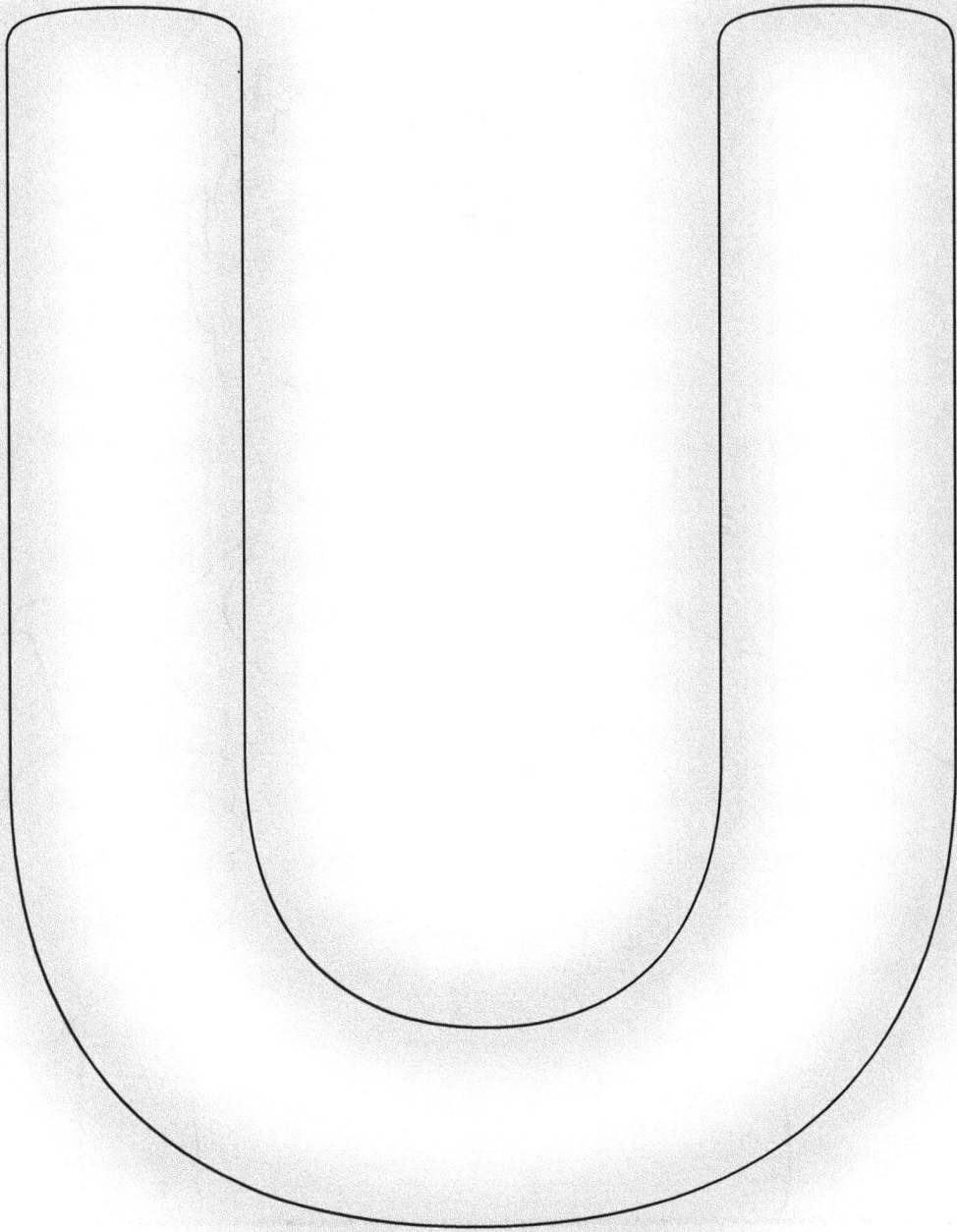

Unity

We are all God's children.

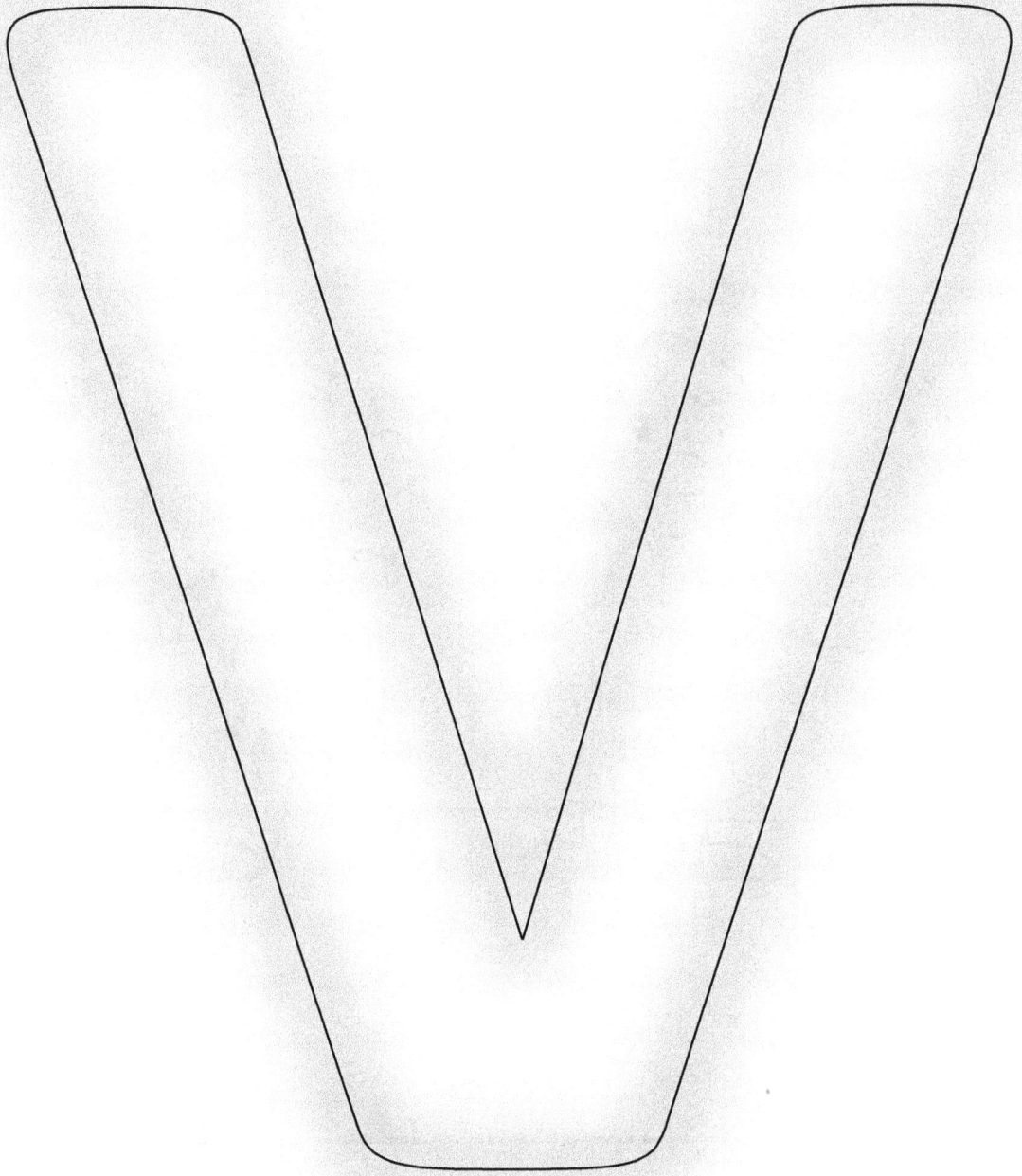

V

Victory

I am victorious through Christ.

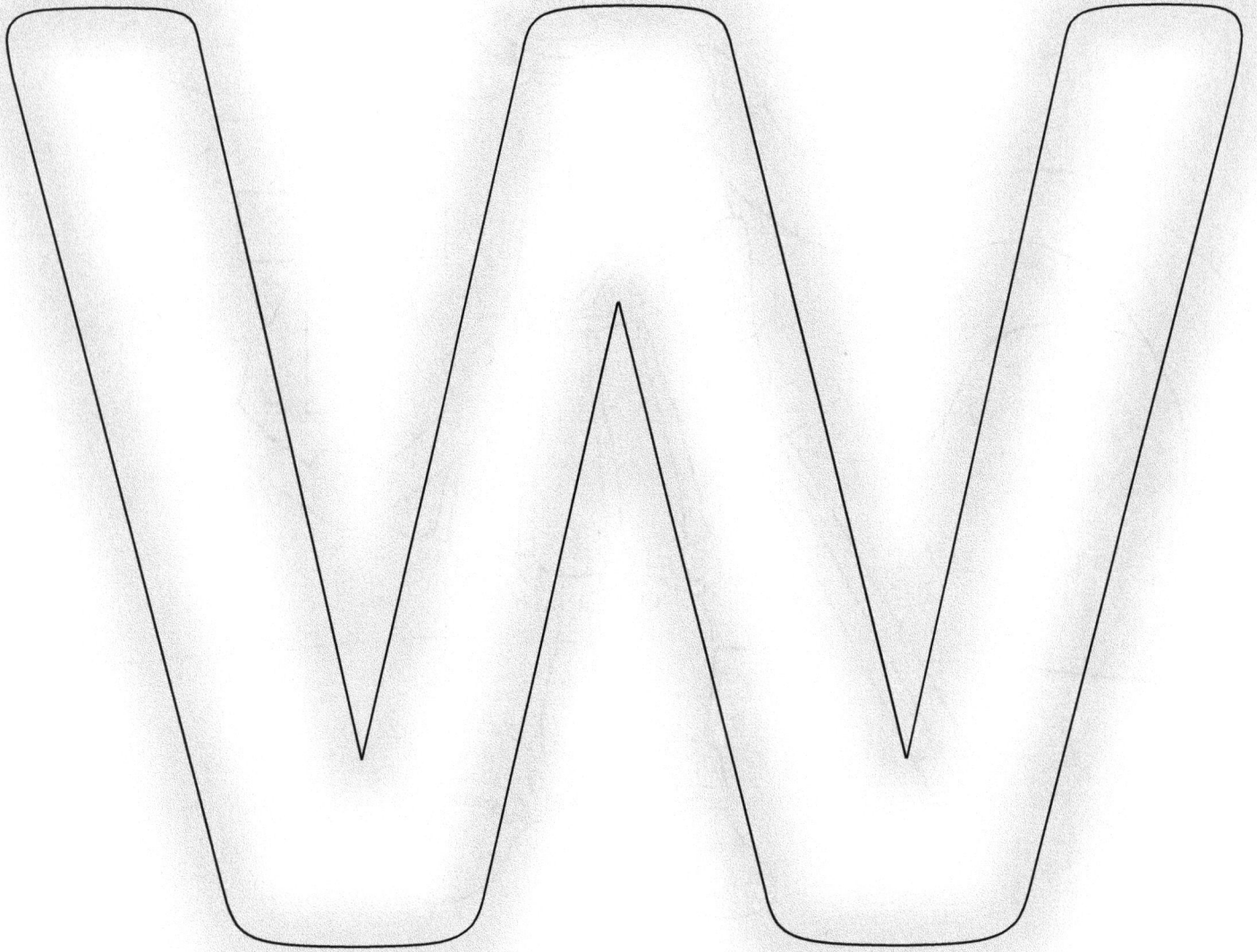

Water

**Jesus went to the
well for water.**

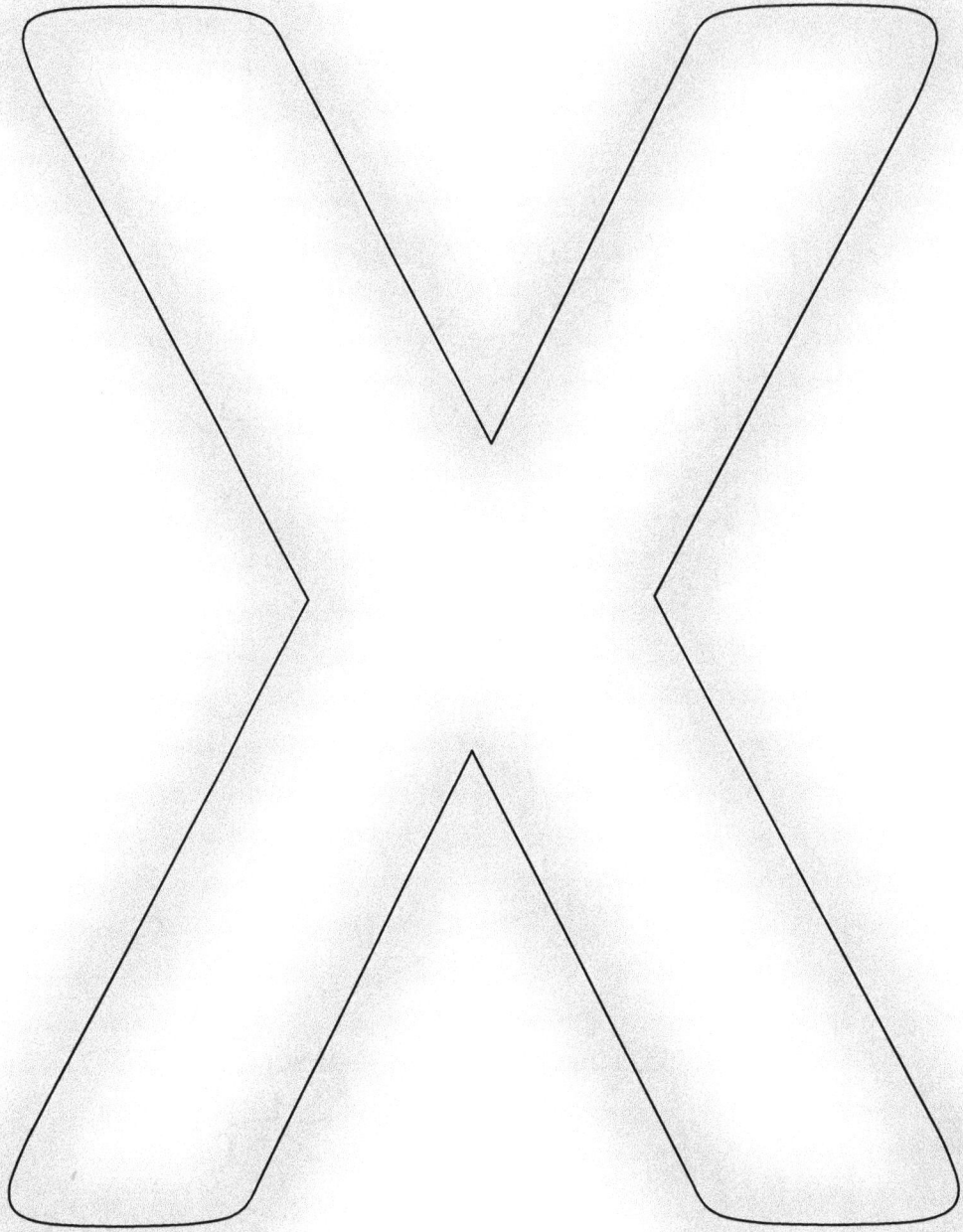

X-Ray

Jesus sees your heart.

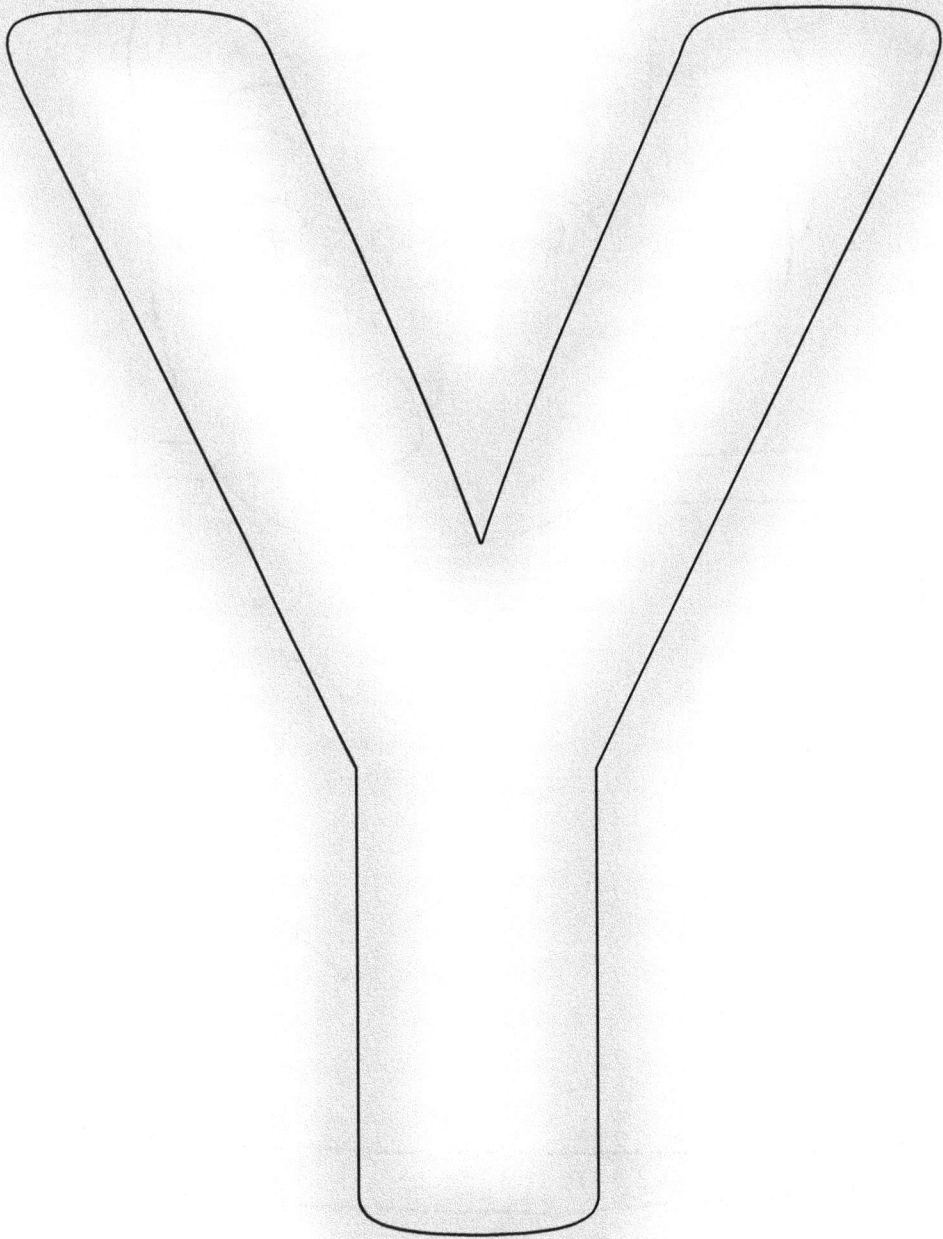

Y

Yahweh

He is the Creator of all.

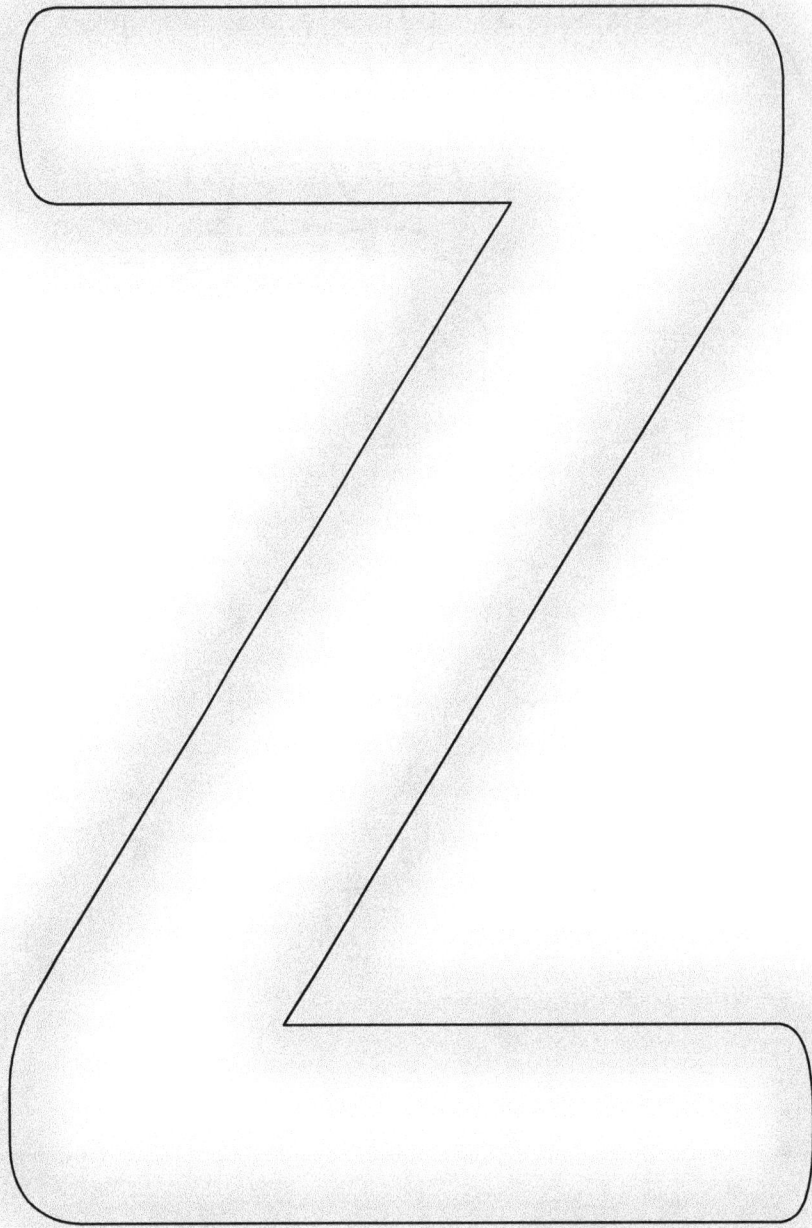

Z

Zacchaeus

Jesus told Zacchaeus to come down from the sycamore tree.

www.ingramcontent.com/pod-product-compliance
Lightning Source LLC
Chambersburg PA
CBHW080532030426
42337CB00023B/4701